Life is an adventure.

It's not the destination we
reach that's most rewarding.
It's the journey along the way.

So **Write It Down!** & treasure
the memory forever . . .

Barbara Morina

Day: _____ Date: _____

Daily Devotions
A Prayer Journal

The weather today: _____
_____

Today I feel: _____
_____
_____

Today I am grateful for: _____
_____
_____
_____

Inspirations, prayer, scriptures, quotes: _____
_____
_____
_____
_____

I said a special prayer for: _____
_____
_____

Prayer(s) answered (comfort, peace, love and miracles): _____
_____
_____
_____

Donations of the Heart (acts of kindness, sharing, caring, and forgiveness): _____
_____
_____
_____

What I would like to see happen tomorrow (Goals, ideas, etc.): _____
_____
_____
_____
_____

"Coincidence is God's way of remaining anonymous"

 The *"Write It Down"*™ Series

Reflections / Notes: _____

_____

_____

_____

_____

_____

_____

_____

_____

_____

_____

_____

_____

_____

_____

_____

_____

_____

_____

_____

_____

_____

_____

_____

_____

_____

_____

_____

Daily Devotions
A Prayer Journal

Day: _____   Date: _____

Daily Devotions
A Prayer Journal

The weather today: _____
_____

Today I feel: _____
_____
_____

Today I am grateful for: _____
_____
_____
_____

Inspirations, prayer, scriptures, quotes: _____
_____
_____
_____

I said a special prayer for: _____
_____
_____

Prayer(s) answered (comfort, peace, love and miracles): _____
_____
_____
_____

Donations of the Heart (acts of kindness, sharing, caring, and forgiveness): _____
_____
_____
_____

What I would like to see happen tomorrow (Goals, ideas, etc.): _____
_____
_____
_____

"Coincidence is God's way of remaining anonymous"

Reflections / Notes:

Day: _____ Date: _____

The weather today: _____
_____

Today I feel: _____
_____
_____

Today I am grateful for: _____
_____
_____

Inspirations, prayer, scriptures, quotes: _____
_____
_____
_____

I said a special prayer for: _____
_____
_____
_____

Prayer(s) answered (comfort, peace, love and miracles): _____
_____
_____
_____

Donations of the Heart (acts of kindness, sharing, caring, and forgiveness): _____
_____
_____
_____

What I would like to see happen tomorrow (Goals, ideas, etc.): _____
_____
_____
_____

"Coincidence is God's way of remaining anonymous"

Reflections / Notes:

Daily Devotions
A Prayer Journal

Day: _____ Date: _____

The weather today: _____
_____

Today I feel: _____
_____
_____

Today I am grateful for: _____
_____
_____

Inspirations, prayer, scriptures, quotes: _____
_____
_____
_____

I said a special prayer for: _____
_____
_____

Prayer(s) answered (comfort, peace, love and miracles): _____
_____
_____
_____

Donations of the Heart (acts of kindness, sharing, caring, and forgiveness): _____
_____
_____

What I would like to see happen tomorrow (Goals, ideas, etc.): _____
_____
_____
_____

"Coincidence is God's way of remaining anonymous"

Reflections / Notes:

Daily Devotions
A Prayer Journal

Day: _____ Date: _____

The weather today: _____
_____

Today I feel: _____
_____
_____

Today I am grateful for: _____
_____
_____

Inspirations, prayer, scriptures, quotes: _____
_____
_____
_____

I said a special prayer for: _____
_____
_____

Prayer(s) answered (comfort, peace, love and miracles): _____
_____
_____
_____

Donations of the Heart (acts of kindness, sharing, caring, and forgiveness): _____
_____
_____
_____

What I would like to see happen tomorrow (Goals, ideas, etc.): _____
_____
_____
_____

"Coincidence is God's way of remaining anonymous"

Reflections / Notes:_____

_____

_____

_____

_____

_____

_____

_____

_____

_____

_____

_____

_____

_____

_____

_____

_____

_____

_____

_____

_____

_____

_____

_____

_____

_____

_____

_____

_____

_____

_____

_____

Day: _____ Date: _____

The weather today: _____

_____

Today I feel: _____

_____

_____

Today I am grateful for: _____

_____

_____

_____

Inspirations, prayer, scriptures, quotes: _____

_____

_____

_____

I said a special prayer for: _____

_____

_____

Prayer(s) answered (comfort, peace, love and miracles): _____

_____

_____

_____

Donations of the Heart (acts of kindness, sharing, caring, and forgiveness): _____

_____

_____

_____

What I would like to see happen tomorrow (Goals, ideas, etc.): _____

_____

_____

_____

"Coincidence is God's way of remaining anonymous"

Reflections / Notes: _____

Daily Devotions
A Prayer Journal

_____
_____
_____
_____
_____
_____
_____
_____
_____
_____
_____
_____
_____
_____
_____
_____
_____
_____
_____
_____
_____
_____
_____
_____
_____
_____
_____
_____
_____
_____
_____
_____
_____
_____

Day: _____ Date: _____

The weather today: _____
_____

Today I feel: _____
_____
_____

Today I am grateful for: _____
_____
_____

Inspirations, prayer, scriptures, quotes: _____
_____
_____

I said a special prayer for: _____
_____
_____

Prayer(s) answered (comfort, peace, love and miracles): _____
_____
_____

Donations of the Heart (acts of kindness, sharing, caring, and forgiveness): _____
_____
_____

What I would like to see happen tomorrow (Goals, ideas, etc.): _____
_____
_____

"Coincidence is God's way of remaining anonymous"

Daily Devotions
A Prayer Journal

Reflections / Notes: _____

Daily Devotions
A Prayer Journal

_____
_____
_____
_____
_____
_____
_____
_____
_____
_____
_____
_____
_____
_____
_____
_____
_____
_____
_____
_____
_____
_____
_____
_____
_____
_____
_____
_____
_____
_____

Day: _____ Date: _____

The weather today: _____

_____

Today I feel: _____

_____

_____

Today I am grateful for: _____

_____

_____

_____

Inspirations, prayer, scriptures, quotes: _____

_____

HOLY
BIBLE

_____

_____

I said a special prayer for: _____

_____

_____

_____

Prayer(s) answered (comfort, peace, love and miracles): _____

_____

_____

_____

_____

Donations of the Heart (acts of kindness, sharing, caring, and forgiveness): _____

_____

_____

_____

_____

What I would like to see happen tomorrow (Goals, ideas, etc.): _____

_____

_____

_____

_____

"Coincidence is God's way of remaining anonymous"

Reflections / Notes: _____

Daily Devotions
A Prayer Journal

_____

_____

_____

_____

_____

_____

_____

_____

_____

_____

_____

_____

_____

_____

_____

_____

_____

_____

_____

_____

_____

_____

_____

_____

_____

_____

_____

_____

_____

Day: _____ Date: _____

The weather today: _____

_____

Today I feel: _____

_____

_____

Today I am grateful for: _____

_____

_____

Inspirations, prayer, scriptures, quotes: _____

_____

_____

I said a special prayer for: _____

_____

Prayer(s) answered (comfort, peace, love and miracles): _____

_____

_____

Donations of the Heart (acts of kindness, sharing, caring, and forgiveness): _____

_____

_____

What I would like to see happen tomorrow (Goals, ideas, etc.): _____

_____

_____

"Coincidence is God's way of remaining anonymous"

Reflections / Notes: _____

Daily Devotions
A Prayer Journal

_____
_____
_____
_____
_____
_____
_____
_____
_____
_____
_____
_____
_____
_____
_____
_____
_____
_____
_____
_____
_____
_____
_____
_____
_____
_____
_____
_____
_____
_____
_____
_____
_____
_____

Day: _____   Date: _____

The weather today: _____
_____

Today I feel: _____
_____
_____

Today I am grateful for: _____
_____
_____
_____

Inspirations, prayer, scriptures, quotes: _____
_____
_____
_____

I said a special prayer for: _____
_____
_____

Prayer(s) answered (comfort, peace, love and miracles): _____
_____
_____
_____

Donations of the Heart (acts of kindness, sharing, caring, and forgiveness): _____
_____
_____
_____

What I would like to see happen tomorrow (Goals, ideas, etc.): _____
_____
_____
_____

"Coincidence is God's way of remaining anonymous"

Reflections / Notes:

Daily Devotions
A Prayer Journal

Day: _____, Date: _____

The weather today: _____

_____

Today I feel: _____

_____

_____

Today I am grateful for: _____

_____

_____

Inspirations, prayer, scriptures, quotes: _____

_____

_____

_____

I said a special prayer for: _____

_____

_____

Prayer(s) answered (comfort, peace, love and miracles): ___

_____

_____

Donations of the Heart (acts of kindness, sharing, caring, and forgiveness): _____

_____

_____

What I would like to see happen tomorrow (Goals, ideas, etc.): _____

_____

_____

_____

"Coincidence is God's way of remaining anonymous"

Reflections / Notes:

Daily Devotions
A Prayer Journal

Day: _____ Date: _____

The weather today: _____
_____

Today I feel: _____
_____
_____

Today I am grateful for: _____
_____
_____

Inspirations, prayer, scriptures, quotes: _____
_____
_____
_____

I said a special prayer for: _____
_____
_____

Prayer(s) answered (comfort, peace, love and miracles): ____
_____
_____
_____

Donations of the Heart (acts of kindness, sharing, caring, and forgiveness): _____
_____
_____
_____

What I would like to see happen tomorrow (Goals, ideas, etc.): _____
_____
_____
_____
_____

"Coincidence is God's way of remaining anonymous"

Reflections / Notes: _____

Daily Devotions
A Prayer Journal

Day: _____   Date: _____

The weather today: _____
_____

Today I feel: _____
_____
_____

Today I am grateful for: _____
_____
_____
_____

Inspirations, prayer, scriptures, quotes: _____
_____
_____
_____

I said a special prayer for: _____
_____
_____
_____

Prayer(s) answered (comfort, peace, love and miracles): _____
_____
_____
_____

Donations of the Heart (acts of kindness, sharing, caring, and forgiveness): _____
_____
_____
_____

What I would like to see happen tomorrow (Goals, ideas, etc.): _____
_____
_____
_____

"Coincidence is God's way of remaining anonymous"

Reflections / Notes: _____

Daily Devotions
A Prayer Journal

Day: _____ Date: _____

The weather today: _____
_____

Today I feel: _____
_____
_____

Today I am grateful for: _____
_____
_____

Inspirations, prayer, scriptures, quotes: _____
_____
_____
_____

I said a special prayer for: _____
_____
_____

Prayer(s) answered (comfort, peace, love and miracles): _____
_____
_____
_____

Donations of the Heart (acts of kindness, sharing, caring, and forgiveness): _____
_____
_____
_____

What I would like to see happen tomorrow (Goals, ideas, etc.): _____
_____
_____
_____

"Coincidence is God's way of remaining anonymous"

Reflections / Notes:

Day: _____ Date: _____

The weather today: _____

_____

Today I feel: _____

_____

_____

Today I am grateful for: _____

_____

_____

Inspirations, prayer, scriptures, quotes: _____

_____

HOLY BIBLE

_____

I said a special prayer for: _____

_____

_____

Prayer(s) answered (comfort, peace, love and miracles): _____

_____

_____

Donations of the Heart (acts of kindness, sharing, caring, and forgiveness): _____

_____

_____

_____

What I would like to see happen tomorrow (Goals, ideas, etc.): _____

_____

_____

_____

"Coincidence is God's way of remaining anonymous"

Reflections / Notes:

Daily Devotions
A Prayer Journal

Day: _____   Date: _____

The weather today: _____

_____

Today I feel: _____

_____

_____

Today I am grateful for: _____

_____

_____

Inspirations, prayer, scriptures, quotes: _____

_____

_____

_____

I said a special prayer for: _____

_____

_____

Prayer(s) answered (comfort, peace, love and miracles): __

_____

_____

_____

Donations of the Heart (acts of kindness, sharing, caring, and forgiveness): _____

_____

_____

_____

What I would like to see happen tomorrow (Goals, ideas, etc.): _____

_____

_____

_____

"Coincidence is God's way of remaining anonymous"

Reflections / Notes: _____

Daily Devotions
A Prayer Journal

Day: _____ Date: _____

The weather today: _____
_____

Today I feel: _____
_____
_____

Today I am grateful for: _____
_____
_____

Inspirations, prayer, scriptures, quotes: _____
_____
_____
_____

I said a special prayer for: _____
_____
_____

Prayer(s) answered (comfort, peace, love and miracles): _____
_____
_____

Donations of the Heart (acts of kindness, sharing, caring, and forgiveness): _____
_____
_____

What I would like to see happen tomorrow (Goals, ideas, etc.): _____
_____
_____
_____

"Coincidence is God's way of remaining anonymous"

Reflections / Notes:

_____

_____

_____

_____

_____

_____

_____

_____

_____

_____

_____

_____

_____

_____

_____

_____

_____

_____

_____

_____

_____

_____

_____

_____

_____

_____

_____

_____

_____

Day: _____   Date: _____

The weather today: _____

_____

Today I feel: _____

_____

_____

Today I am grateful for: _____

_____

_____

_____

Inspirations, prayer, scriptures, quotes: _____

_____

_____

_____

I said a special prayer for: _____

_____

_____

Prayer(s) answered (comfort, peace, love and miracles): _____

_____

_____

_____

Donations of the Heart (acts of kindness, sharing, caring, and forgiveness): _____

_____

_____

_____

What I would like to see happen tomorrow (Goals, ideas, etc.): _____

_____

_____

_____

"Coincidence is God's way of remaining anonymous"

© 1999 Journals Unlimited, Inc., Bay City, MI The "Write It Down"™ Series

Reflections / Notes:

Daily Devotions
A Prayer Journal

Day: _____ Date: _____

Daily Devotions
A Prayer Journal

The weather today: _____
_____

Today I feel: _____
_____
_____
_____

Today I am grateful for: _____
_____
_____
_____

Inspirations, prayer, scriptures, quotes: _____
_____
_____
_____

I said a special prayer for: _____
_____
_____

Prayer(s) answered (comfort, peace, love and miracles): _____
_____
_____

Donations of the Heart (acts of kindness, sharing, caring, and forgiveness): _____
_____
_____
_____

What I would like to see happen tomorrow (Goals, ideas, etc.): _____
_____
_____
_____

"Coincidence is God's way of remaining anonymous"

Reflections / Notes:

Daily Devotions
A Prayer Journal

Day: _____ Date: _____

The weather today: _____
_____

Today I feel: _____
_____
_____

Today I am grateful for: _____
_____
_____
_____

Inspirations, prayer, scriptures, quotes: _____
_____
_____
_____

I said a special prayer for: _____
_____
_____

Prayer(s) answered (comfort, peace, love and miracles): ___
_____
_____

Donations of the Heart (acts of kindness, sharing, caring, and forgiveness): _____
_____
_____
_____

What I would like to see happen tomorrow (Goals, ideas, etc.): _____
_____
_____
_____

"Coincidence is God's way of remaining anonymous"

Reflections / Notes:

_____

Daily Devotions
A Prayer Journal

Day: _____   Date: _____

Daily Devotions
A Prayer Journal

The weather today: _____
_____

Today I feel: _____
_____
_____

Today I am grateful for: _____
_____
_____

Inspirations, prayer, scriptures, quotes: _____
_____
_____
_____

I said a special prayer for: _____
_____
_____

Prayer(s) answered (comfort, peace, love and miracles): ____
_____
_____

Donations of the Heart (acts of kindness, sharing, caring, and forgiveness): _____
_____
_____

What I would like to see happen tomorrow (Goals, ideas, etc.): _____
_____
_____

"Coincidence is God's way of remaining anonymous"

Reflections / Notes: _____

Daily Devotions
A Prayer Journal

Day: _____   Date: _____

The weather today: _____
_____

Today I feel: _____
_____
_____

Today I am grateful for: _____
_____
_____

Inspirations, prayer, scriptures, quotes: _____
_____
_____
_____

I said a special prayer for: _____
_____
_____

Prayer(s) answered (comfort, peace, love and miracles): _____
_____
_____
_____

Donations of the Heart (acts of kindness, sharing, caring, and forgiveness): _____
_____
_____
_____

What I would like to see happen tomorrow (Goals, ideas, etc.): _____
_____
_____
_____

"Coincidence is God's way of remaining anonymous"

Reflections / Notes:

Day: _____ Date: _____

The weather today: _____
_____

Today I feel: _____
_____
_____

Today I am grateful for: _____
_____
_____

Inspirations, prayer, scriptures, quotes: _____
_____
_____
_____

I said a special prayer for: _____
_____
_____

Prayer(s) answered (comfort, peace, love and miracles): ___
_____
_____

Donations of the Heart (acts of kindness, sharing, caring, and forgiveness): _____
_____
_____

What I would like to see happen tomorrow (Goals, ideas, etc.): _____
_____
_____
_____

"Coincidence is God's way of remaining anonymous"

Reflections / Notes:

Day: _____ Date: _____

The weather today: _____

_____

Today I feel: _____

_____

_____

Today I am grateful for: _____

_____

_____

Inspirations, prayer, scriptures, quotes: _____

_____

_____

_____

I said a special prayer for: _____

_____

_____

Prayer(s) answered (comfort, peace, love and miracles): _____

_____

_____

_____

Donations of the Heart (acts of kindness, sharing, caring, and forgiveness): _____

_____

_____

_____

What I would like to see happen tomorrow (Goals, ideas, etc.): _____

_____

_____

_____

_____

"Coincidence is God's way of remaining anonymous"

Reflections / Notes:

Daily Devotions
A Prayer Journal

Day: _____ Date: _____

Daily Devotions
A Prayer Journal

The weather today: _____
_____

Today I feel: _____
_____
_____

Today I am grateful for: _____
_____
_____

Inspirations, prayer, scriptures, quotes: _____
_____
_____
_____

I said a special prayer for: _____
_____
_____

Prayer(s) answered (comfort, peace, love and miracles): _____
_____
_____

Donations of the Heart (acts of kindness, sharing, caring, and forgiveness): _____
_____
_____

What I would like to see happen tomorrow (Goals, ideas, etc.): _____
_____
_____

"Coincidence is God's way of remaining anonymous"

Reflections / Notes:

Day: _____ Date: _____

The weather today: _____
_____

Today I feel: _____
_____
_____

Today I am grateful for: _____
_____
_____
_____

Inspirations, prayer, scriptures, quotes: _____
_____
_____
_____

I said a special prayer for: _____
_____
_____

Prayer(s) answered (comfort, peace, love and miracles): _____
_____
_____

Donations of the Heart (acts of kindness, sharing, caring, and forgiveness): _____
_____
_____

What I would like to see happen tomorrow (Goals, ideas, etc.): _____
_____
_____
_____

"Coincidence is God's way of remaining anonymous"

Reflections /, Notes:_____

Daily Devotions
A Prayer Journal

Day: _____ Date: _____

The weather today: _____
_____

Today I feel: _____
_____
_____

Today I am grateful for: _____
_____
_____

Inspirations, prayer, scriptures, quotes: _____
_____
_____
_____

I said a special prayer for: _____
_____
_____

Prayer(s) answered (comfort, peace, love and miracles): _____
_____
_____

Donations of the Heart (acts of kindness, sharing, caring, and forgiveness): _____
_____
_____
_____

What I would like to see happen tomorrow (Goals, ideas, etc.): _____
_____
_____
_____

"Coincidence is God's way of remaining anonymous"

Reflections / Notes:

Daily Devotions
A Prayer Journal

Day: _____ Date: _____

The weather today: _____
_____

Today I feel: _____
_____
_____

Today I am grateful for: _____
_____
_____
_____

Inspirations, prayer, scriptures, quotes: _____
_____
_____
_____

I said a special prayer for: _____
_____
_____

Prayer(s) answered (comfort, peace, love and miracles): _____
_____
_____
_____

Donations of the Heart (acts of kindness, sharing, caring, and forgiveness): _____
_____
_____
_____

What I would like to see happen tomorrow (Goals, ideas, etc.): _____
_____
_____
_____

"Coincidence is God's way of remaining anonymous"

Reflections / Notes:

Daily Devotions
A Prayer Journal

Day: _____'_____ Date: _____

The weather today: _____
_____

Today I feel: _____
_____
_____

Today I am grateful for: _____
_____
_____
_____

Inspirations, prayer, scriptures, quotes: _____
_____
_____
_____
_____

I said a special prayer for: _____
_____
_____

Prayer(s) answered (comfort, peace, love and miracles): _____
_____
_____
_____

Donations of the Heart (acts of kindness, sharing, caring, and forgiveness): _____
_____
_____
_____

What I would like to see happen tomorrow (Goals, ideas, etc.): _____
_____
_____
_____
_____

"Coincidence is God's way of remaining anonymous"

Reflections / Notes:

Day: _____ Date: _____

The weather today: _____
_____

Today I feel: _____
_____
_____

Today I am grateful for: _____
_____
_____
_____

Inspirations, prayer, scriptures, quotes: _____
_____
_____
_____

I said a special prayer for: _____
_____
_____

Prayer(s) answered (comfort, peace, love and miracles): _____
_____
_____
_____

Donations of the Heart (acts of kindness, sharing, caring, and forgiveness): _____
_____
_____
_____

What I would like to see happen tomorrow (Goals, ideas, etc.): _____
_____
_____
_____
_____

"Coincidence is God's way of remaining anonymous"

Reflections / Notes:_____

_____

_____

_____

_____

_____

_____

_____

_____

_____

_____

_____

_____

_____

_____

_____

_____

_____

_____

_____

_____

_____

_____

_____

_____

_____

_____

_____

_____

_____

_____

_____

Daily Devotions
A Prayer Journal

Day: _____ Date: _____

The weather today: _____
_____

Today I feel: _____
_____
_____

Today I am grateful for: _____
_____
_____

Inspirations, prayer, scriptures, quotes: _____
_____
_____
_____

I said a special prayer for: _____
_____
_____

Prayer(s) answered (comfort, peace, love and miracles): _____
_____
_____

Donations of the Heart (acts of kindness, sharing, caring, and forgiveness): _____
_____
_____

What I would like to see happen tomorrow (Goals, ideas, etc.): _____
_____
_____
_____

"Coincidence is God's way of remaining anonymous"

Reflections / Notes:

Day: _____ Date: _____

The weather today: _____
_____

Today I feel: _____
_____
_____

Today I am grateful for: _____
_____
_____

Inspirations, prayer, scriptures, quotes: _____
_____
_____
_____

I said a special prayer for: _____
_____
_____

Prayer(s) answered (comfort, peace, love and miracles): ____
_____
_____

Donations of the Heart (acts of kindness, sharing, caring, and forgiveness): ____
_____
_____
_____

What I would like to see happen tomorrow (Goals, ideas, etc.): ____
_____
_____
_____
_____

"Coincidence is God's way of remaining anonymous"

Reflections / Notes:

Day: _____ Date: _____

The weather today: _____
_____

Today I feel: _____
_____
_____

Today I am grateful for: _____
_____
_____

Inspirations, prayer, scriptures, quotes: _____
_____
_____
_____

I said a special prayer for: _____
_____
_____

Prayer(s) answered (comfort, peace, love and miracles): _____
_____
_____
_____

Donations of the Heart (acts of kindness, sharing, caring, and forgiveness): _____
_____
_____
_____

What I would like to see happen tomorrow (Goals, ideas, etc.): _____
_____
_____
_____

"Coincidence is God's way of remaining anonymous"

Reflections / Notes: _____

Daily Devotions
A Prayer Journal

_____

_____

_____

_____

_____

_____

_____

_____

_____

_____

_____

_____

_____

_____

_____

_____

_____

_____

_____

_____

_____

_____

_____

_____

_____

_____

_____

_____

_____

_____

_____

Day: _____   Date: _____

The weather today: _____
_____

Today I feel: _____
_____
_____

Today I am grateful for: _____
_____
_____
_____

Inspirations, prayer, scriptures, quotes: _____
_____
_____
_____

I said a special prayer for: _____
_____
_____

Prayer(s) answered (comfort, peace, love and miracles): _____
_____
_____
_____

Donations of the Heart (acts of kindness, sharing, caring, and forgiveness): _____
_____
_____
_____

What I would like to see happen tomorrow (Goals, ideas, etc.): _____
_____
_____
_____

"Coincidence is God's way of remaining anonymous"

Reflections / Notes:

Day: _____   Date: _____

The weather today: _____
_____

Today I feel: _____
_____
_____

Today I am grateful for: _____
_____
_____

Inspirations, prayer, scriptures, quotes: _____
_____
_____
_____

I said a special prayer for: _____
_____
_____

Prayer(s) answered (comfort, peace, love and miracles): _____
_____
_____
_____

Donations of the Heart (acts of kindness, sharing, caring, and forgiveness): _____
_____
_____

What I would like to see happen tomorrow (Goals, ideas, etc.): _____
_____
_____
_____

"Coincidence is God's way of remaining anonymous"

© 1999 Journals Unlimited, Inc., Bay City, MI The "Write It Down"™ Series

Reflections / Notes:

Day: _____   Date: _____

The weather today: _____
_____

Today I feel: _____
_____
_____

Today I am grateful for: _____
_____
_____

Inspirations, prayer, scriptures, quotes: _____
_____
_____
_____

I said a special prayer for: _____
_____
_____

Prayer(s) answered (comfort, peace, love and miracles): ____
_____
_____
_____

Donations of the Heart (acts of kindness, sharing, caring, and forgiveness): ____
_____
_____
_____

What I would like to see happen tomorrow (Goals, ideas, etc.): ____
_____
_____
_____

"Coincidence is God's way of remaining anonymous"

Reflections / Notes:_____

Daily Devotions
A Prayer Journal

Day: _____ Date: _____

Daily Devotions
A Prayer Journal

The weather today: _____
_____

Today I feel: _____
_____
_____

Today I am grateful for: _____
_____
_____

Inspirations, prayer, scriptures, quotes: _____
_____
_____
_____

I said a special prayer for: _____
_____
_____

Prayer(s) answered (comfort, peace, love and miracles): _____
_____
_____
_____

Donations of the Heart (acts of kindness, sharing, caring, and forgiveness): _____
_____
_____
_____

What I would like to see happen tomorrow (Goals, ideas, etc.): _____
_____
_____
_____

"Coincidence is God's way of remaining anonymous"

© 1999 Journals Unlimited, Inc., Bay City, MI The "Write It Down"™ Series

Reflections / Notes:

Day: _____ Date: _____

The weather today: _____
_____

Today I feel: _____
_____
_____
_____

Today I am grateful for: _____
_____
_____
_____

Inspirations, prayer, scriptures, quotes: _____
_____
_____
_____

I said a special prayer for: _____
_____
_____

Prayer(s) answered (comfort, peace, love and miracles): ___
_____
_____
_____

Donations of the Heart (acts of kindness, sharing, caring, and forgiveness): ___
_____
_____
_____

What I would like to see happen tomorrow (Goals, ideas, etc.): ___
_____
_____
_____

"Coincidence is God's way of remaining anonymous"

Reflections / Notes:

Day: _____ Date: _____

The weather today: _____
_____

Today I feel: _____
_____
_____

Today I am grateful for: _____
_____
_____

Inspirations, prayer, scriptures, quotes: _____
_____
_____
_____

I said a special prayer for: _____
_____
_____

Prayer(s) answered (comfort, peace, love and miracles): ____
_____
_____
_____

Donations of the Heart (acts of kindness, sharing, caring, and forgiveness): _____
_____
_____
_____

What I would like to see happen tomorrow (Goals, ideas, etc.): ____
_____
_____
_____

"Coincidence is God's way of remaining anonymous"

Reflections / Notes:

Daily Devotions
A Prayer Journal

Day: _____ Date: _____

The weather today: _____
_____

Today I feel: _____
_____
_____

Today I am grateful for: _____
_____
_____

Inspirations, prayer, scriptures, quotes: _____
_____
_____
_____

I said a special prayer for: _____
_____
_____

Prayer(s) answered (comfort, peace, love and miracles): _____
_____
_____
_____

Donations of the Heart (acts of kindness, sharing, caring, and forgiveness): _____
_____
_____
_____

What I would like to see happen tomorrow (Goals, ideas, etc.): _____
_____
_____
_____

"Coincidence is God's way of remaining anonymous"

Reflections / Notes:

Day: _____ Date: _____

The weather today: _____
_____

Today I feel: _____
_____
_____

Today I am grateful for: _____
_____
_____
_____

Inspirations, prayer, scriptures, quotes: _____
_____
_____
_____
_____

I said a special prayer for: _____
_____
_____

Prayer(s) answered (comfort, peace, love and miracles): _____
_____
_____
_____

Donations of the Heart (acts of kindness, sharing, caring, and forgiveness): _____
_____
_____
_____

What I would like to see happen tomorrow (Goals, ideas, etc.): _____
_____
_____
_____

"Coincidence is God's way of remaining anonymous"

Reflections / Notes:

Day: _____ Date: _____

The weather today: _____

_____

Today I feel: _____

_____

_____

Today I am grateful for: _____

_____

_____

Inspirations, prayer, scriptures, quotes: _____

_____

_____

_____

I said a special prayer for: _____

_____

_____

Prayer(s) answered (comfort, peace, love and miracles): ____

_____

_____

_____

Donations of the Heart (acts of kindness, sharing, caring, and forgiveness): _____

_____

_____

_____

What I would like to see happen tomorrow (Goals, ideas, etc.): _____

_____

_____

_____

"Coincidence is God's way of remaining anonymous"

Reflections / Notes:

Daily Devotions
A Prayer Journal

Day: _____ Date: _____

The weather today: _____
_____

Today I feel: _____
_____
_____

Today I am grateful for: _____
_____
_____

Inspirations, prayer, scriptures, quotes: _____
_____
_____
_____

I said a special prayer for: _____
_____
_____

Prayer(s) answered (comfort, peace, love and miracles): ___
_____
_____

Donations of the Heart (acts of kindness, sharing, caring, and forgiveness): _____
_____
_____
_____

What I would like to see happen tomorrow (Goals, ideas, etc.): _____
_____
_____
_____

"Coincidence is God's way of remaining anonymous"

Reflections / Notes:

Day: _____ Date: _____

The weather today: _____

Today I feel: _____

_____

_____

Today I am grateful for: _____

_____

_____

Inspirations, prayer, scriptures, quotes: _____

_____

_____

_____

I said a special prayer for: _____

_____

_____

Prayer(s) answered (comfort, peace, love and miracles): _____

_____

_____

Donations of the Heart (acts of kindness, sharing, caring, and forgiveness): _____

_____

_____

What I would like to see happen tomorrow (Goals, ideas, etc.): _____

_____

_____

"Coincidence is God's way of remaining anonymous"

Reflections / Notes: _____

Daily Devotions
A Prayer Journal

_____
_____
_____
_____
_____
_____
_____
_____
_____
_____
_____
_____
_____
_____
_____
_____
_____
_____
_____
_____
_____
_____
_____
_____
_____
_____
_____
_____
_____
_____
_____

Day: _____ Date: _____

The weather today: _____
_____

Today I feel: _____
_____
_____

Today I am grateful for: _____
_____
_____

Inspirations, prayer, scriptures, quotes: _____
_____
_____
_____

I said a special prayer for: _____
_____
_____

Prayer(s) answered (comfort, peace, love and miracles): _____
_____
_____
_____

Donations of the Heart (acts of kindness, sharing, caring, and forgiveness): _____
_____
_____
_____

What I would like to see happen tomorrow (Goals, ideas, etc.): _____
_____
_____
_____

"Coincidence is God's way of remaining anonymous"

Reflections / Notes:

Day: _____ Date: _____

Daily Devotions
A Prayer Journal

The weather today: _____
_____

Today I feel: _____
_____
_____

Today I am grateful for: _____
_____
_____

Inspirations, prayer, scriptures, quotes: _____
_____
_____
_____

I said a special prayer for: _____
_____
_____

Prayer(s) answered (comfort, peace, love and miracles): ___
_____
_____
_____

Donations of the Heart (acts of kindness, sharing, caring, and forgiveness): _____
_____
_____
_____

What I would like to see happen tomorrow (Goals, ideas, etc.): _____
_____
_____
_____

"Coincidence is God's way of remaining anonymous"

© 1999 Journals Unlimited, Inc., Bay City, MI The "Write It Down"™ Series

Reflections / Notes:

Daily Devotions
A Prayer Journal

Day: _____ Date: _____

The weather today: _____
_____

Today I feel: _____
_____
_____

Today I am grateful for: _____
_____
_____

Inspirations, prayer, scriptures, quotes: _____
_____
_____
_____

I said a special prayer for: _____
_____
_____

Prayer(s) answered (comfort, peace, love and miracles): ____
_____
_____

Donations of the Heart (acts of kindness, sharing, caring, and forgiveness): _____
_____
_____

What I would like to see happen tomorrow (Goals, ideas, etc.): _____
_____
_____
_____

"Coincidence is God's way of remaining anonymous"

Daily Devotions
A Prayer Journal

Reflections / Notes:

Day: _____ Date: _____

The weather today: _____
_____

Today I feel: _____
_____
_____

Today I am grateful for: _____
_____
_____
_____

Inspirations, prayer, scriptures, quotes: _____
_____
_____
_____

I said a special prayer for: _____
_____
_____

Prayer(s) answered (comfort, peace, love and miracles): _____
_____
_____

Donations of the Heart (acts of kindness, sharing, caring, and forgiveness): _____
_____
_____

What I would like to see happen tomorrow (Goals, ideas, etc.): _____
_____
_____
_____

"Coincidence is God's way of remaining anonymous"

Reflections / Notes: _____

Daily Devotions
A Prayer Journal

Day: _____ Date: _____

The weather today: _____

Today I feel: _____
_____
_____

Today I am grateful for: _____
_____
_____

Inspirations, prayer, scriptures, quotes: _____
_____
_____
_____

I said a special prayer for: _____
_____
_____

Prayer(s) answered (comfort, peace, love and miracles): _____
_____
_____

Donations of the Heart (acts of kindness, sharing, caring, and forgiveness): _____
_____
_____

What I would like to see happen tomorrow (Goals, ideas, etc.): _____
_____
_____
_____

"Coincidence is God's way of remaining anonymous"

Reflections / Notes:_____

Daily Devotions
A Prayer Journal

Day: _____   Date: _____

The weather today: _____

Today I feel: _____

_____

_____

Today I am grateful for: _____

_____

_____

Inspirations, prayer, scriptures, quotes: _____

_____

_____

_____

I said a special prayer for: _____

_____

_____

Prayer(s) answered (comfort, peace, love and miracles): _____

_____

_____

_____

Donations of the Heart (acts of kindness, sharing, caring, and forgiveness): _____

_____

_____

_____

What I would like to see happen tomorrow (Goals, ideas, etc.): _____

_____

_____

_____

"Coincidence is God's way of remaining anonymous"

Reflections / Notes:

Day: _____ Date: _____

The weather today: _____
_____

Today I feel: _____
_____
_____

Today I am grateful for: _____
_____
_____

Inspirations, prayer, scriptures, quotes: _____
_____
_____
_____

I said a special prayer for: _____
_____
_____

Prayer(s) answered (comfort, peace, love and miracles): _____
_____
_____

Donations of the Heart (acts of kindness, sharing, caring, and forgiveness): _____
_____
_____
_____

What I would like to see happen tomorrow (Goals, ideas, etc.): _____
_____
_____
_____

"Coincidence is God's way of remaining anonymous"

Reflections / Notes: _____

Daily Devotions
A Prayer Journal

Day: _____ Date: _____

The weather today: _____
_____

Today I feel: _____
_____
_____

Today I am grateful for: _____
_____
_____

Inspirations, prayer, scriptures, quotes: _____
_____
_____
_____

I said a special prayer for: _____
_____
_____

Prayer(s) answered (comfort, peace, love and miracles): _____
_____
_____

Donations of the Heart (acts of kindness, sharing, caring, and forgiveness): _____
_____
_____

What I would like to see happen tomorrow (Goals, ideas, etc.): _____
_____
_____
_____

"Coincidence is God's way of remaining anonymous"

Reflections / Notes:

Day: _____ Date: _____

The weather today: _____

_____

Today I feel: _____

_____

_____

Today I am grateful for: _____

_____

_____

Inspirations, prayer, scriptures, quotes: _____

_____

_____

_____

I said a special prayer for: _____

_____

_____

Prayer(s) answered (comfort, peace, love and miracles): _____

_____

_____

_____

Donations of the Heart (acts of kindness, sharing, caring, and forgiveness): _____

_____

_____

_____

What I would like to see happen tomorrow (Goals, ideas, etc.): _____

_____

_____

_____

"Coincidence is God's way of remaining anonymous"

Reflections / Notes:

Day: _____   Date: _____

The weather today: _____
_____

Today I feel: _____
_____
_____

Today I am grateful for: _____
_____
_____

Inspirations, prayer, scriptures, quotes: _____
_____
_____
_____

I said a special prayer for: _____
_____
_____

Prayer(s) answered (comfort, peace, love and miracles): ___
_____
_____
_____

Donations of the Heart (acts of kindness, sharing, caring, and forgiveness): _____
_____
_____
_____

What I would like to see happen tomorrow (Goals, ideas, etc.): _____
_____
_____
_____

"Coincidence is God's way of remaining anonymous"

Reflections / Notes:

Daily Devotions
A Prayer Journal

Day: _____ Date: _____

The weather today: _____
_____

Today I feel: _____
_____
_____

Today I am grateful for: _____
_____
_____

Inspirations, prayer, scriptures, quotes: _____
_____
_____
_____

I said a special prayer for: _____
_____
_____

Prayer(s) answered (comfort, peace, love and miracles): ____
_____
_____
_____

Donations of the Heart (acts of kindness, sharing, caring, and forgiveness): ____
_____
_____
_____

What I would like to see happen tomorrow (Goals, ideas, etc.): ____
_____
_____
_____

"Coincidence is God's way of remaining anonymous"

Reflections / Notes: _____

Daily Devotions
A Prayer Journal

_____
_____
_____
_____
_____
_____
_____
_____
_____
_____
_____
_____
_____
_____
_____
_____
_____
_____
_____
_____
_____
_____
_____
_____
_____
_____
_____
_____

Day: _____ Date: _____

The weather today: _____

Today I feel: _____
_____
_____

Today I am grateful for: _____
_____
_____
_____

Inspirations, prayer, scriptures, quotes: _____
_____
_____
_____
_____

I said a special prayer for: _____
_____
_____
_____

Prayer(s) answered (comfort, peace, love and miracles): ___
_____
_____
_____

Donations of the Heart (acts of kindness, sharing, caring, and forgiveness): ____
_____
_____
_____

What I would like to see happen tomorrow (Goals, ideas, etc.): ___
_____
_____
_____
_____

"Coincidence is God's way of remaining anonymous"

Reflections / Notes:

Day: _____ Date: _____

Daily Devotions
A Prayer Journal

The weather today: _____
_____

Today I feel: _____
_____
_____

Today I am grateful for: _____
_____
_____

Inspirations, prayer, scriptures, quotes: _____
_____
_____
_____

I said a special prayer for: _____
_____
_____

Prayer(s) answered (comfort, peace, love and miracles): _____
_____
_____

Donations of the Heart (acts of kindness, sharing, caring, and forgiveness): _____
_____
_____
_____

What I would like to see happen tomorrow (Goals, ideas, etc.): _____
_____
_____
_____

"Coincidence is God's way of remaining anonymous"

Reflections / Notes:

Day: _____ Date: _____

The weather today: _____
_____

Today I feel: _____
_____
_____

Today I am grateful for: _____
_____
_____
_____

Inspirations, prayer, scriptures, quotes: _____
_____
_____
_____

I said a special prayer for: _____
_____
_____

Prayer(s) answered (comfort, peace, love and miracles): _____
_____
_____
_____

Donations of the Heart (acts of kindness, sharing, caring, and forgiveness): _____
_____
_____
_____

What I would like to see happen tomorrow (Goals, ideas, etc.): _____
_____
_____
_____
_____

"Coincidence is God's way of remaining anonymous"

Reflections / Notes: _____

Daily Devotions
A Prayer Journal

_____
_____
_____
_____
_____
_____
_____
_____
_____
_____
_____
_____
_____
_____
_____
_____
_____
_____
_____
_____
_____
_____
_____
_____
_____
_____
_____
_____
_____
_____

Day: _____   Date: _____

The weather today: _____
_____

Today I feel: _____
_____
_____

Today I am grateful for: _____
_____
_____

Inspirations, prayer, scriptures, quotes: _____
_____
_____
_____

I said a special prayer for: _____
_____
_____

Prayer(s) answered (comfort, peace, love and miracles): _____
_____
_____
_____

Donations of the Heart (acts of kindness, sharing, caring, and forgiveness): _____
_____
_____
_____

What I would like to see happen tomorrow (Goals, ideas, etc.): _____
_____
_____
_____
_____

"Coincidence is God's way of remaining anonymous"

Reflections / Notes:

Day: _____ Date: _____

Daily Devotions
A Prayer Journal

The weather today: _____
_____

Today I feel: _____
_____
_____
_____

Today I am grateful for: _____
_____
_____
_____

Inspirations, prayer, scriptures, quotes: _____
_____
_____
_____
_____

I said a special prayer for: _____
_____
_____
_____

Prayer(s) answered (comfort, peace, love and miracles): ____
_____
_____
_____
_____

Donations of the Heart (acts of kindness, sharing, caring, and forgiveness): _____
_____
_____
_____
_____

What I would like to see happen tomorrow (Goals, ideas, etc.): _____
_____
_____
_____
_____

"Coincidence is God's way of remaining anonymous"

Reflections / Notes: _____

Daily Devotions
A Prayer Journal

Day: _____ Date: _____

The weather today: _____
_____

Today I feel: _____
_____
_____
_____

Today I am grateful for: _____
_____
_____
_____

Inspirations, prayer, scriptures, quotes: _____
_____
_____
_____
_____

I said a special prayer for: _____
_____
_____
_____

Prayer(s) answered (comfort, peace, love and miracles): _____
_____
_____
_____

Donations of the Heart (acts of kindness, sharing, caring, and forgiveness): _____
_____
_____
_____

What I would like to see happen tomorrow (Goals, ideas, etc.): _____
_____
_____
_____

"Coincidence is God's way of remaining anonymous"

Reflections / Notes: _____

_____

_____

_____

_____

_____

_____

_____

_____

_____

_____

_____

_____

_____

_____

_____

_____

_____

_____

_____

_____

_____

_____

_____

_____

_____

_____

_____

_____

_____

_____

_____

Daily Devotions
A Prayer Journal

Day: _____ Date: _____

The weather today: _____

Today I feel: _____
_____
_____

Today I am grateful for: _____
_____
_____

Inspirations, prayer, scriptures, quotes: _____
_____
_____
_____

I said a special prayer for: _____
_____
_____

Prayer(s) answered (comfort, peace, love and miracles): _____
_____
_____

Donations of the Heart (acts of kindness, sharing, caring, and forgiveness): _____
_____
_____

What I would like to see happen tomorrow (Goals, ideas, etc.): _____
_____
_____
_____

"Coincidence is God's way of remaining anonymous"

Reflections / Notes:

Day: _____ Date: _____

The weather today: _____

_____

Today I feel: _____

_____

_____

Today I am grateful for: _____

_____

_____

Inspirations, prayer, scriptures, quotes: _____

_____

_____

_____

I said a special prayer for: _____

_____

_____

Prayer(s) answered (comfort, peace, love and miracles): ___

_____

_____

_____

Donations of the Heart (acts of kindness, sharing, caring, and forgiveness): ___

_____

_____

_____

What I would like to see happen tomorrow (Goals, ideas, etc.): ___

_____

_____

_____

"Coincidence is God's way of remaining anonymous"

© 1999 Journals Unlimited, Inc., Bay City, MI The "Write It Down" Series

Reflections / Notes: _____

Daily Devotions
A Prayer Journal

Day: _____ Date: _____

The weather today: _____
_____

Today I feel: _____
_____
_____

Today I am grateful for: _____
_____
_____
_____

Inspirations, prayer, scriptures, quotes: _____
_____
_____
_____
_____

I said a special prayer for: _____
_____
_____

Prayer(s) answered (comfort, peace, love and miracles): _____
_____
_____
_____

Donations of the Heart (acts of kindness, sharing, caring, and forgiveness): _____
_____
_____
_____

What I would like to see happen tomorrow (Goals, ideas, etc.): _____
_____
_____
_____
_____

"Coincidence is God's way of remaining anonymous"

Reflections / Notes:

Day: _____'_____ Date:_____

The weather today: _____
_____

Today I feel: _____
_____

Today I am grateful for: _____
_____
_____

Inspirations, prayer, scriptures, quotes: _____
_____
_____
_____

I said a special prayer for: _____
_____
_____

Prayer(s) answered (comfort, peace, love and miracles): ___
_____
_____

Donations of the Heart (acts of kindness, sharing, caring, and forgiveness): ____
_____
_____

What I would like to see happen tomorrow (Goals, ideas, etc.): ____
_____
_____
_____

"Coincidence is God's way of remaining anonymous"

Reflections / Notes:

Day: _____ Date: _____

The weather today: _____
_____

Today I feel: _____
_____
_____

Today I am grateful for: _____
_____
_____
_____

Inspirations, prayer, scriptures, quotes: _____
_____

HOLY BIBLE

_____
_____

I said a special prayer for: _____
_____
_____

Prayer(s) answered (comfort, peace, love and miracles): _____
_____
_____
_____

Donations of the Heart (acts of kindness, sharing, caring, and forgiveness): _____
_____
_____
_____

What I would like to see happen tomorrow (Goals, ideas, etc.): _____
_____
_____
_____

"Coincidence is God's way of remaining anonymous"

Reflections / Notes:

Daily Devotions

A Prayer Journal

The weather today: _____
_____

Today I feel: _____
_____
_____

Today I am grateful for: _____
_____
_____
_____

Inspirations, prayer, scriptures, quotes: _____
_____
_____
_____

I said a special prayer for: _____
_____
_____

Prayer(s) answered (comfort, peace, love and miracles): _____
_____
_____

Donations of the Heart (acts of kindness, sharing, caring, and forgiveness): _____
_____
_____

What I would like to see happen tomorrow (Goals, ideas, etc.): _____
_____
_____
_____

"Coincidence is God's way of remaining anonymous"

Reflections / Notes:

Daily Devotions
A Prayer Journal

Day: _____ Date: _____

The weather today: _____

Today I feel: _____

_____

_____

Today I am grateful for: _____

_____

_____

Inspirations, prayer, scriptures, quotes: _____

_____

_____

_____

I said a special prayer for: _____

_____

_____

Prayer(s) answered (comfort, peace, love and miracles): _____

_____

_____

_____

Donations of the Heart (acts of kindness, sharing, caring, and forgiveness): _____

_____

_____

_____

What I would like to see happen tomorrow (Goals, ideas, etc.): _____

_____

_____

_____

"Coincidence is God's way of remaining anonymous"

Reflections /, Notes:

Daily Devotions
A Prayer Journal

Day: _____ Date: _____

The weather today: _____
_____

Today I feel: _____
_____
_____

Today I am grateful for: _____
_____
_____

Inspirations, prayer, scriptures, quotes: _____
_____
_____
_____
_____

I said a special prayer for: _____
_____
_____

Prayer(s) answered (comfort, peace, love and miracles): _____
_____
_____
_____

Donations of the Heart (acts of kindness, sharing, caring, and forgiveness): _____
_____
_____
_____

What I would like to see happen tomorrow (Goals, ideas, etc.): _____
_____
_____
_____

"Coincidence is God's way of remaining anonymous"

Reflections / Notes:

Daily Devotions
A Prayer Journal

Day: _____ Date: _____

The weather today: _____

Today I feel: _____
_____
_____

Today I am grateful for: _____
_____
_____
_____

Inspirations, prayer, scriptures, quotes: _____
_____
_____
_____

I said a special prayer for: _____
_____
_____

Prayer(s) answered (comfort, peace, love and miracles): _____
_____
_____
_____

Donations of the Heart (acts of kindness, sharing, caring, and forgiveness): _____
_____
_____
_____

What I would like to see happen tomorrow (Goals, ideas, etc.): _____
_____
_____
_____

"Coincidence is God's way of remaining anonymous"

Reflections / Notes:

Day: _____ Date: _____

The weather today: _____

_____

Today I feel: _____

_____

Today I am grateful for: _____

_____

_____

Inspirations, prayer, scriptures, quotes: _____

_____

_____

_____

I said a special prayer for: _____

_____

_____

Prayer(s) answered (comfort, peace, love and miracles): _____

_____

_____

Donations of the Heart (acts of kindness, sharing, caring, and forgiveness): _____

_____

_____

What I would like to see happen tomorrow (Goals, ideas, etc.): _____

_____

_____

_____

"Coincidence is God's way of remaining anonymous"

Reflections / Notes:

Day: _____ Date: _____

The weather today: _____

_____

Today I feel: _____

_____

_____

Today I am grateful for: _____

_____

_____

_____

Inspirations, prayer, scriptures, quotes: _____

_____

_____

_____

_____

I said a special prayer for: _____

_____

_____

Prayer(s) answered (comfort, peace, love and miracles): _____

_____

_____

_____

Donations of the Heart (acts of kindness, sharing, caring, and forgiveness): _____

_____

_____

_____

What I would like to see happen tomorrow (Goals, ideas, etc.): _____

_____

_____

_____

"Coincidence is God's way of remaining anonymous"

Reflections / Notes: _____

Daily Devotions
A Prayer Journal

Daily Devotions

A Prayer Journal

The weather today: _____

_____

Today I feel: _____

_____

_____

Today I am grateful for: _____

_____

_____

Inspirations, prayer, scriptures, quotes: _____

_____

_____

_____

I said a special prayer for: _____

_____

_____

Prayer(s) answered (comfort, peace, love and miracles): _____

_____

_____

Donations of the Heart (acts of kindness, sharing, caring, and forgiveness): _____

_____

_____

_____

What I would like to see happen tomorrow (Goals, ideas, etc.): _____

_____

_____

_____

Reflections / Notes:

Daily Devotions

A Prayer Journal

Day: _____   Date: _____

Daily Devotions
A Prayer Journal

The weather today: _____

Today I feel: _____

_____

_____

Today I am grateful for: _____

_____

_____

Inspirations, prayer, scriptures, quotes: _____

_____

_____

_____

I said a special prayer for: _____

_____

_____

Prayer(s) answered (comfort, peace, love and miracles): _____

_____

_____

Donations of the Heart (acts of kindness, sharing, caring, and forgiveness): _____

_____

_____

_____

What I would like to see happen tomorrow (Goals, ideas, etc.): _____

_____

_____

_____

"Coincidence is God's way of remaining anonymous"

Reflections / Notes:

Day: _____ Date: _____

Daily Devotions
A Prayer Journal

The weather today: _____
_____

Today I feel: _____
_____
_____

Today I am grateful for: _____
_____
_____
_____

Inspirations, prayer, scriptures, quotes: _____
_____
_____
_____

I said a special prayer for: _____
_____
_____

Prayer(s) answered (comfort, peace, love and miracles): _____
_____
_____
_____

Donations of the Heart (acts of kindness, sharing, caring, and forgiveness): _____
_____
_____
_____

What I would like to see happen tomorrow (Goals, ideas, etc.): _____
_____
_____
_____

"Coincidence is God's way of remaining anonymous"

Reflections / Notes:_____

Daily Devotions
A Prayer Journal

Day: _____ Date: _____

The weather today: _____
_____

Today I feel: _____
_____
_____

Today I am grateful for: _____
_____
_____

Inspirations, prayer, scriptures, quotes: _____
_____
_____

I said a special prayer for: _____
_____

Prayer(s) answered (comfort, peace, love and miracles): _____
_____
_____

Donations of the Heart (acts of kindness, sharing, caring, and forgiveness): _____
_____
_____

What I would like to see happen tomorrow (Goals, ideas, etc.): _____
_____
_____
_____

"Coincidence is God's way of remaining anonymous"

Reflections / Notes:

Daily Devotions
A Prayer Journal

Day: _____ Date: _____

The weather today: _____
_____

Today I feel: _____
_____
_____

Today I am grateful for: _____
_____
_____

Inspirations, prayer, scriptures, quotes: _____
_____
_____

I said a special prayer for: _____
_____
_____

Prayer(s) answered (comfort, peace, love and miracles): _____
_____
_____

Donations of the Heart (acts of kindness, sharing, caring, and forgiveness): _____
_____
_____

What I would like to see happen tomorrow (Goals, ideas, etc.): _____
_____
_____
_____

"Coincidence is God's way of remaining anonymous"

© 1999 Journals Unlimited, Inc., Bay City, MI The "Write It Down"™ Series

Reflections / Notes: _____

Daily Devotions
A Prayer Journal

_____

Day: _____ Date: _____

Daily Devotions
A Prayer Journal

The weather today: _____
_____

Today I feel: _____
_____
_____

Today I am grateful for: _____
_____
_____
_____

Inspirations, prayer, scriptures, quotes: _____
_____
_____
_____

I said a special prayer for: _____
_____
_____

Prayer(s) answered (comfort, peace, love and miracles): _____
_____
_____
_____

Donations of the Heart (acts of kindness, sharing, caring, and forgiveness): _____
_____
_____
_____

What I would like to see happen tomorrow (Goals, ideas, etc.): _____
_____
_____
_____

"Coincidence is God's way of remaining anonymous"

Reflections / Notes:

Daily Devotions
A Prayer Journal

Day: _____ Date: _____

Daily Devotions
A Prayer Journal

The weather today: _____

Today I feel: _____

_____

_____

Today I am grateful for: _____

_____

_____

Inspirations, prayer, scriptures, quotes: _____

HOLY BIBLE

_____

_____

I said a special prayer for: _____

_____

_____

Prayer(s) answered (comfort, peace, love and miracles): ____

_____

_____

Donations of the Heart (acts of kindness, sharing, caring, and forgiveness): _____

_____

_____

_____

What I would like to see happen tomorrow (Goals, ideas, etc.): _____

_____

_____

_____

"Coincidence is God's way of remaining anonymous"

Reflections / Notes: _____

Daily Devotions

A Prayer Journal

Day: _____ Date: _____

The weather today: _____
_____

Today I feel: _____
_____
_____

Today I am grateful for: _____
_____
_____
_____

Inspirations, prayer, scriptures, quotes: _____
_____
_____
_____

I said a special prayer for: _____
_____
_____

Prayer(s) answered (comfort, peace, love and miracles): ___
_____
_____
_____

Donations of the Heart (acts of kindness, sharing, caring, and forgiveness): _____
_____
_____
_____

What I would like to see happen tomorrow (Goals, ideas, etc.): _____
_____
_____
_____

"Coincidence is God's way of remaining anonymous"

Reflections / Notes:

Day: _____ Date: _____

The weather today: _____
_____

Today I feel: _____
_____
_____

Today I am grateful for: _____
_____
_____
_____

Inspirations, prayer, scriptures, quotes: _____
_____
_____
_____

I said a special prayer for: _____
_____
_____

Prayer(s) answered (comfort, peace, love and miracles): _____
_____
_____

Donations of the Heart (acts of kindness, sharing, caring, and forgiveness): _____
_____
_____
_____

What I would like to see happen tomorrow (Goals, ideas, etc.): _____
_____
_____
_____

"Coincidence is God's way of remaining anonymous"

Reflections / Notes:

Daily Devotions
A Prayer Journal

Day: _____ Date: _____

The weather today: _____

_____

Today I feel: _____

_____

_____

Today I am grateful for: _____

_____

_____

_____

Inspirations, prayer, scriptures, quotes: _____

_____

_____

_____

I said a special prayer for: _____

_____

_____

Prayer(s) answered (comfort, peace, love and miracles): ____

_____

_____

_____

Donations of the Heart (acts of kindness, sharing, caring, and forgiveness): ____

_____

_____

_____

What I would like to see happen tomorrow (Goals, ideas, etc.): ____

_____

_____

_____

"Coincidence is God's way of remaining anonymous"

Reflections / Notes:

Daily Devotions
A Prayer Journal

Day: _____ Date: _____

The weather today: _____
_____

Today I feel: _____
_____
_____

Today I am grateful for: _____
_____
_____
_____

Inspirations, prayer, scriptures, quotes: _____
_____
_____
_____

I said a special prayer for: _____
_____
_____

Prayer(s) answered (comfort, peace, love and miracles): _____
_____
_____
_____

Donations of the Heart (acts of kindness, sharing, caring, and forgiveness): _____
_____
_____
_____

What I would like to see happen tomorrow (Goals, ideas, etc.): _____
_____
_____
_____

"Coincidence is God's way of remaining anonymous"

© 1999 Journals Unlimited, Inc., Bay City, MI The "Write It Down" Series

Reflections / Notes:

Day: _____ Date: _____

The weather today: _____
_____
_____

Today I feel: _____
_____
_____

Today I am grateful for: _____
_____
_____
_____

Inspirations, prayer, scriptures, quotes: _____
_____
_____
_____

I said a special prayer for: _____
_____
_____

Prayer(s) answered (comfort, peace, love and miracles): _____
_____
_____
_____

Donations of the Heart (acts of kindness, sharing, caring, and forgiveness): _____
_____
_____
_____

What I would like to see happen tomorrow (Goals, ideas, etc.): _____
_____
_____
_____

"Coincidence is God's way of remaining anonymous"

Reflections / Notes:

Daily Devotions
A Prayer Journal

Day: _____ Date:_____

The weather today: _____

_____

Today I feel: _____

_____

_____

Today I am grateful for: _____

_____

_____

_____

Inspirations, prayer, scriptures, quotes: _____

_____

_____

_____

_____

I said a special prayer for: _____

_____

_____

_____

Prayer(s) answered (comfort, peace, love and miracles): _____

_____

_____

_____

Donations of the Heart (acts of kindness, sharing, caring, and forgiveness): _____

_____

_____

_____

What I would like to see happen tomorrow (Goals, ideas, etc.): _____

_____

_____

_____

_____

"Coincidence is God's way of remaining anonymous"

Reflections / Notes: _____

Daily Devotions
A Prayer Journal

Day: _____   Date:_____

The weather today: _____

_____

Today I feel: _____

_____

_____

Today I am grateful for: _____

_____

_____

_____

Inspirations, prayer, scriptures, quotes: _____

_____

_____

_____

I said a special prayer for: _____

_____

_____

_____

Prayer(s) answered (comfort, peace, love and miracles): _____

_____

_____

_____

Donations of the Heart (acts of kindness, sharing, caring, and forgiveness): _____

_____

_____

_____

What I would like to see happen tomorrow (Goals, ideas, etc.): _____

_____

_____

_____

"Coincidence is God's way of remaining anonymous"

Reflections /, Notes:

Daily Devotions
A Prayer Journal

Day: _____ Date: _____

The weather today: _____
_____

Today I feel: _____
_____
_____

Today I am grateful for: _____
_____
_____

Inspirations, prayer, scriptures, quotes: _____
_____
_____
_____

I said a special prayer for: _____
_____
_____

Prayer(s) answered (comfort, peace, love and miracles): _____
_____
_____
_____

Donations of the Heart (acts of kindness, sharing, caring, and forgiveness): _____
_____
_____
_____

What I would like to see happen tomorrow (Goals, ideas, etc.): _____
_____
_____
_____

"Coincidence is God's way of remaining anonymous"

Reflections / Notes:

Day: _____ Date: _____

The weather today: _____
_____

Today I feel: _____
_____

Today I am grateful for: _____
_____
_____
_____

Inspirations, prayer, scriptures, quotes: _____
_____
_____
_____

I said a special prayer for: _____
_____
_____

Prayer(s) answered (comfort, peace, love and miracles): _____
_____
_____
_____

Donations of the Heart (acts of kindness, sharing, caring, and forgiveness): _____
_____
_____
_____

What I would like to see happen tomorrow (Goals, ideas, etc.): _____
_____
_____
_____

"Coincidence is God's way of remaining anonymous"

Reflections / Notes:

Daily Devotions
A Prayer Journal

 The "*Write It Down*"™ Series

Day: _____ Date: _____

The weather today: _____

Today I feel: _____
_____
_____

Today I am grateful for: _____
_____
_____

Inspirations, prayer, scriptures, quotes: _____
_____
_____
_____

I said a special prayer for: _____
_____
_____

Prayer(s) answered (comfort, peace, love and miracles): ____
_____
_____
_____

Donations of the Heart (acts of kindness, sharing, caring, and forgiveness): _____
_____
_____
_____

What I would like to see happen tomorrow (Goals, ideas, etc.): _____
_____
_____
_____

"Coincidence is God's way of remaining anonymous"

Reflections / Notes: _____

Day: _____ Date: _____

The weather today: _____
_____

Today I feel: _____
_____
_____

Today I am grateful for: _____
_____
_____
_____

Inspirations, prayer, scriptures, quotes: _____
_____
_____
_____

I said a special prayer for: _____
_____
_____

Prayer(s) answered (comfort, peace, love and miracles): _____
_____
_____
_____

Donations of the Heart (acts of kindness, sharing, caring, and forgiveness): _____
_____
_____
_____

What I would like to see happen tomorrow (Goals, ideas, etc.): _____
_____
_____
_____

"Coincidence is God's way of remaining anonymous"

Reflections / Notes:

Day: _____ Date: _____

The weather today: _____

_____

Today I feel: _____

_____

_____

Today I am grateful for: _____

_____

_____

_____

Inspirations, prayer, scriptures, quotes: _____

_____

_____

_____

I said a special prayer for: _____

_____

_____

Prayer(s) answered (comfort, peace, love and miracles): _____

_____

_____

_____

Donations of the Heart (acts of kindness, sharing, caring, and forgiveness): _____

_____

_____

_____

What I would like to see happen tomorrow (Goals, ideas, etc.): _____

_____

_____

_____

"Coincidence is God's way of remaining anonymous"

Reflections / Notes:

Daily Devotions
A Prayer Journal

Day: _____   Date: _____

The weather today: _____

_____

Today I feel: _____

_____

_____

Today I am grateful for: _____

_____

_____

_____

Inspirations, prayer, scriptures, quotes: _____

_____

_____

_____

I said a special prayer for: _____

_____

_____

_____

Prayer(s) answered (comfort, peace, love and miracles): _____

_____

_____

_____

Donations of the Heart (acts of kindness, sharing, caring, and forgiveness): _____

_____

_____

_____

What I would like to see happen tomorrow (Goals, ideas, etc.): _____

_____

_____

_____

_____

"Coincidence is God's way of remaining anonymous"

Reflections / Notes:

Day: _____ Date: _____

The weather today: _____
_____

Today I feel: _____
_____
_____

Today I am grateful for: _____
_____
_____

Inspirations, prayer, scriptures, quotes: _____
_____
_____
_____

I said a special prayer for: _____
_____
_____

Prayer(s) answered (comfort, peace, love and miracles): ____
_____
_____

Donations of the Heart (acts of kindness, sharing, caring, and forgiveness): _____
_____
_____

What I would like to see happen tomorrow (Goals, ideas, etc.): _____
_____
_____
_____

"Coincidence is God's way of remaining anonymous"

Reflections / Notes:

Daily Devotions
A Prayer Journal

Day: _____ Date: _____

The weather today: _____
_____

Today I feel: _____
_____
_____

Today I am grateful for: _____
_____
_____
_____

Inspirations, prayer, scriptures, quotes: _____
_____
_____
_____

I said a special prayer for: _____
_____
_____

Prayer(s) answered (comfort, peace, love and miracles): ___
_____
_____
_____

Donations of the Heart (acts of kindness, sharing, caring, and forgiveness): _____
_____
_____
_____

What I would like to see happen tomorrow (Goals, ideas, etc.): _____
_____
_____
_____
_____

"Coincidence is God's way of remaining anonymous"

Reflections / Notes:

Daily Devotions

A Prayer Journal

The weather today: _____

Today I feel: _____

_____

Today I am grateful for: _____

_____

_____

_____

Inspirations, prayer, scriptures, quotes: _____

HOLY BIBLE

_____

_____

I said a special prayer for: _____

_____

_____

Prayer(s) answered (comfort, peace, love and miracles): _____

_____

_____

Donations of the Heart (acts of kindness, sharing, caring, and forgiveness): _____

_____

_____

_____

What I would like to see happen tomorrow (Goals, ideas, etc.): _____

_____

_____

_____

"Coincidence is God's way of remaining anonymous"

Reflections / Notes:

Day: _____ Date: _____

The weather today: _____

_____

Today I feel: _____

_____

_____

Today I am grateful for: _____

_____

_____

_____

Inspirations, prayer, scriptures, quotes: _____

_____

_____

_____

I said a special prayer for: _____

_____

_____

Prayer(s) answered (comfort, peace, love and miracles): _____

_____

_____

_____

Donations of the Heart (acts of kindness, sharing, caring, and forgiveness): _____

_____

_____

_____

What I would like to see happen tomorrow (Goals, ideas, etc.): _____

_____

_____

_____

_____

"Coincidence is God's way of remaining anonymous"

Reflections / Notes:

Daily Devotions
A Prayer Journal

Day: _____ Date: _____

The weather today: _____
_____

Today I feel: _____
_____
_____

Today I am grateful for: _____
_____
_____
_____

Inspirations, prayer, scriptures, quotes: _____
_____
_____
_____

I said a special prayer for: _____
_____
_____

Prayer(s) answered (comfort, peace, love and miracles): _____
_____
_____
_____

Donations of the Heart (acts of kindness, sharing, caring, and forgiveness): _____
_____
_____
_____

What I would like to see happen tomorrow (Goals, ideas, etc.): _____
_____
_____
_____

"Coincidence is God's way of remaining anonymous"

Reflections / Notes: _____

Daily Devotions
A Prayer Journal

Day: _____ Date: _____

The weather today: _____

Today I feel: _____
_____
_____

Today I am grateful for: _____
_____
_____
_____

Inspirations, prayer, scriptures, quotes: _____
_____
_____
_____

I said a special prayer for: _____
_____
_____
_____

Prayer(s) answered (comfort, peace, love and miracles): _____
_____
_____
_____

Donations of the Heart (acts of kindness, sharing, caring, and forgiveness): _____
_____
_____
_____

What I would like to see happen tomorrow (Goals, ideas, etc.): _____
_____
_____
_____

"Coincidence is God's way of remaining anonymous"

© 1999 Journals Unlimited, Inc., Bay City, MI The "Write It Down" Series

Reflections / Notes:

Day: _____ Date: _____

The weather today: _____
_____

Today I feel: _____
_____
_____

Today I am grateful for: _____
_____
_____
_____

Inspirations, prayer, scriptures, quotes: _____
_____
_____
_____

I said a special prayer for: _____
_____
_____

Prayer(s) answered (comfort, peace, love and miracles): _____
_____
_____

Donations of the Heart (acts of kindness, sharing, caring, and forgiveness): _____
_____
_____
_____

What I would like to see happen tomorrow (Goals, ideas, etc.): _____
_____
_____
_____

"Coincidence is God's way of remaining anonymous"

Reflections / Notes: _____

_____

_____

_____

_____

_____

_____

_____

_____

_____

_____

_____

_____

_____

_____

_____

_____

_____

_____

_____

_____

_____

_____

_____

_____

_____

_____

_____

_____

Daily Devotions
A Prayer Journal